TECUMSEH
Don Gutteridge

ISBN 0 88750 201 6 (hardcover)
ISBN 0 88750 202 4 (softcover)

Cover courtesy Stark Museum of Art
Design by Michael Macklem

Printed in Canada

PUBLISHED IN CANADA BY OBERON PRESS

This book is the fourth part of a tetralogy entitled *Dreams and Visions: The Land*. The first three were: *Riel: A Poem for Voices* (1968), *Coppermine: The Quest for North* (1973) and *Borderlands* (1975).

DEATH AT QUEBEC (THE SEIGNEUR TELLS IT)

At first
the sun burned
our pink skin

warmth and
brandy-laughter in
the long house
Good Cheer, they said

our prayers
scented the
green chapel-wood

in there
I could smell
                God

    (with *him*: our
    muskets make the
    silence jump back—
    it grows again
    seamless/self-healing—
    striding thru
    drifts to the
    brown doe
    dead against a
    hump of snow,
    back-broken like a stick
    oh the blood-sweet
    dark venison of her

our beards drip
with it, *his*
mouth: a wound)

Every year a child
grows out of her
like a tuber, a
corn-blight sucking
nine months on the
stalk of her, but
ruptured spores breed:
(wind diseased) the
stem of her green once

once cradling my lust
I rooted in her
summered on her thighs
she caught the rain of
my sperm   O God the
ground gave way and we
both survived

Last night. . . again
she took it in her clay
crotch (like a carrot)
even my lust couldn't heal

    her prayers
    in the evening
    are sweet breathing
    are incense falling:
    my ears speak

8

These sons of mine
(I saw them red-skinned
birth-blood still on them
pink worms
crawled out of that
clay seam   only her
screams gave my ear
pain, made it all
at least animal)
where will they find
an image of knowing?

I see them now
on rivers of noise
on the Ottawa
on the Richelieu
brains worn smooth
with endless paddling
their souls gone
to the beaver or
some darker furring
among the bronzed
grease-glistening whores
spread-eagled on every
hump of granite)

And my fat daughters,
leeches that feed
on my love 'til
the bone gleams
pain shines

)

This land will
not breed corn
but flies thrive
drink the cool
sun in

I have one son,
he tills the
brutal soil
fumbles prayers on
his thick tongue
obeys me with his body
breaks ground lustily:
but there is no marriage
of sun and earth here,
he cannot beat the fields
into submission, his
rage withers the corn

    clay is stubborn
    loves pain

"Pray to God," his mother said

But he too has looked for Him
behind the shadow
under the ice
in the blind sun

There he is now!
He's broken the share
snapped it cross-grain
fingers too calloused
to feel the seam,
his tongue moves easy
in a furrow of curses

I will tell him!

But these dreams:

    red-skinned squaw
    on the domed snow
    weakening where
    thighs cross
    articulate
    O God   the gun
    slides
        blood-wet
    into the sweet
    dark deer-meat
            of her. . . .

Are these woods a
shadow around me or
in me? the sun
is thin with
shining thru them

11

This granite is older
than our first bone
is seamed with myth
with hieroglyphic runings
sealed by a silence
that stilled the
first and vital Word
(conspiracy of
                    sun/earth
and condoning sea)

This earth
made its covenant
with universal darkness
long before the God of
Abraham broke Chaos
with his lance
of light

Year by year
I sit
in the sun's thinning
my age growing around
me, the shadow
lengthens, grows
no darker, no
more light is let
thru the trees,

the dreams persist
but do not be-
come a dream,
will not give me
life or death,
I watch my son
abuse the earth
he sprang from,
see his mother
stiffen because the
yearly child no
longer oils her
seam with blood,
think of my sons
dying   graveless
the wind praying
over their bones—
somewhere a savage whore
tuberous-bellied
full of black
spore the earth
will spit back at her
will spit back at me

because I sit
year by year
watch the seasons
rot and revive

3

The sun is
keen today
against the leather
of my skin,
is clean

and casts
no shadow

out or in

14

THE BISHOP'S APOLOGY

Our attics teem with
the night-breathings
of animals so dark
daylight passes thru them.
By candleflame, at the altar,
I've seen their shadows
flick in the eyes of priests

What are they?
And what do they do
but wait to occupy
the spaces I can't see?

They are gargoyles,
the burnt-out plots
of past mythologies,
like all of us
they have endured
beyond the meaning
of their lives, the
grotesqueries
(old old men
in whose mouths the
language coagulates)

We have made a clearing
with our axes, our hands
cutting the brush away,
some room for the eyes—
hills, valleys, meadows
they are islands from the
ocean of trees, the
seasons of rolling green,
even here and there (York,
Port Colborne, Goderich)
archipelagoes of
streets   roads   fenced
farms, salvaged
brooks, a church
spire upright in the
angling fierce sun. . .

some pasture for the
eyes, legs, the
hands to heal in:
but the mind needs
room to move and
borders it can graze in
(fences drive the
deer mad, they
flee their own bodies
and the indriven
image of their flesh)

16

The dream of civilization
I carried with me
over the borderless ocean
kept pure in the stink
and rabble of the ship,
have guarded here
against all enemies—
needs room to breathe,
as well, will soon be
feeding on itself
(we are broken animals
crazed by fences—
blood/bones
disconnected symbols
collapsed syntax—
in the daze of
our own speech
we crave the
nightmare dark)

I wake up
in the midst of a
shriek, I want to
keep my mouth open,
let the animals
in, tongue by tongue
they will be
poems bloody
with meaning

17

(but one of the boys
has heard, there will be
explanations enough, and
only Methodists believe
in the confusion of tongues)

We shall build schools
walls and fences
books will be our borderlands
these archipelagoes will
get a handhold
we will drive all the
beasts and creatures
of this dark theology
back and back 'til
the ice spits them up,
there will be such a
babble of tongues, such a
scourging of dead
mythologies Christ Himself
will walk on Lake Ontario
and call it Galilee

It is chill:
the night-wind
rises from the Lake,
Yonge Street is
scrawled with shadow
(one could drown
in that calligraphy)

From the pantry
comes the chatter
of invisible teeth. . . .

19

PIONEERS: GIRL/WOMAN

Released, she
lets the wind
divide her, it
slides thru
double-winged
(flesh feathered)
she rides the in-
divisible earth

Inside
the log-walls
tighten, stir
her thin bones
lengthening
without consent

By the pond
the ice is a
mirror you can
see your face in
and that other face
blue and bloodless
below the
current slashes
but cannot
                    break

And the nerve
the ultimate dare:
to fall face-in
and break them
both

GIRL:

I love my mother,
she brings the
water in and
keeps the fire
to make it warm,
under her skin
the blood is
full of sun
rescued from summers/
years I try to
dream about,
her breath fills
the dough that rises
only in this cabin,
she is food
and warmth and things
to put in your dream

Why can't I tell her?
Out there I am
always hungry,
I swallow the
shadows of hawks,
hot spaces in the
snow burn my
delicious skin,
there is no gap
between my leg-
wings (though the
long bones complain)

Out there
I never dream,
or else there's
nothing to tell

WOMAN:

There are so few men
out here: rough loggers,
some trappers, half-
Indians, they all
take their females
like food, pummelling
it with their tongues,
they prefer screams
to cries, like my own
man, and astonished
to see the child
slip out, perfect
as a word.

This one is a
dream of me.
Why do I punish her
with a love
I have constructed
like these log-walls,
this illusion of a
home, this domestic
fiction, when I know
what she has seen
thru the pond-ice,

22

when I too have
only one dream
that some day
will be hers:

this hawk that
screams in the
cage of my brain
as this stranger/
logger/trapper/half-
man pummels the
gap between my
long-boned legs
with a wordless rage

Girl and pond:
her body a
question in the
winter sun,
a signature
the ice writes
on itself
and then erases

23

WOMAN:

Yesterday
one of the hired men
(the half-breed with the stutter)
caught her in the shed,
they were both laughing
as he pulled at her
new breasts and she
kept pointing to his
beet-red horse's thing
"It stutters!" she cried
as her father beat
the animal speechless

Now we shall have to
watch even her brothers

GIRL:

I am starting to
dream: *out there*

My bones are
growing green
logs   somebody
else planted

24

The two seeds
on my chest
have sprouted
little mouths,
they try to
suck on hands,
anybody's hands,
they laugh
when the wind
cries on them

(but we don't fly)

My legs love
the ground and
I can't help it

Between them
a growth, a
new face I
saw in the
pond's shadow—
shaggy and branched:
a mouth within a
wrinkled mouth

it smiled
it wasn't
        me

Then I'll just
close my eyes:
the eagle is
holding the horizon up
with his wing-span
and when the wind comes
he swallows it

WOMAN:

"Labour makes the limbs strong"
I've said that to each of them,
six sons and now this
feather of a girl.
My own hands are as
crooked as the farm
we've chopped out of the
silence (fieldstones
surround us like knuckles)

They say there's a
village now, twenty miles away:
some laughter, maybe
even a man the ground
hasn't made taciturn,
with a voice, a
lilt—the memory
of a dream and the
cadence of flight

26

GIRL:

I don't have to
go out any more,
just shut my eyes
here by the fire
and the wind
bends and divides

I am free at last
from the ground
of my bones,
from the necessity
of flight

WOMAN:

A trapper got her
right here in the cabin,
there by the hearth.
Neither of us wept,
she seemed in a trance,
merely nodded when the
"arrangements" were made:
another cabin, farther north,
further into silence
but the same, and the
brute tongueless
pummelling, the same
cage of dreams

27

GIRL:

I do not dream
at all (like the
trapped creatures
my good man kills
I feed only
on my own pain)

at least that is
what I shall tell
this child come
from the seed
somebody else imagined,
a fine down of
blood still on her
body perfect
as a word

And the blood
has its own dreams
beyond simile. . . .

28

PIONEERS: BOY/MAN

I

My father slashes
at these trees
as if they were
his enemies come
from that other
country to taunt
and challenge,

it is their slow
energy (that same
patience I know
in these bones
feeling their own
lengthwise way
in my flesh)
that maddens his
hands, makes
the axe a
       weapon
his rage a
        strength

In the clearing
he has cut to
fit the only
dream he knows:
his shadow is
a blank face,
the gnarled hands,
back bent
into a wind
that's never there,
legs perpetually
braced, he is
the misshapen tree
of my only
                    nightmare

We mark the
passing years
with charred stumps,
the legbones of
felled trees are
fences, monuments,
casualties of my
father's necessity

30

But the big
trees remain
beyond the clearing
beyond the arc
of hand or axe,
nightmare or dream:
in the coldest day
they etch their grotesquerie
across the whitest sky:

who can read
such signs?

But I was born
here   beneath the
ack pine/beech
white pine/birch
scribbled horizons,
porcelain sun,
two-branched
birds—all the
rawling tree-
creatures of my
childhood's imagining)
but this is not
country, horizons
re not borders,
these root-scarred
attlegrounds are
not fields or farms,
his man whose
beech grows more
range each day

I

is not a father
feeding me dreams
or a language
I can use to
free myself from
him or the trees
or the landscape
binding us both

A song
(in a dream):

> We scourge and plough
> the ground is
> black then brown
> the wheat turns
> green then yellow
> we burn and plough
> the scarred ground
> the wheat renews
> with green and gold
> and harvest-song
> brings round the
> year to turn
> and plough the
> brown autumn, the
> green wish of
> fifteen springs. . .

But these hands
already are old
with ploughing:
what green will renew?

One tree was spared:
the wild apple,
fledgling and
orphaned, my
mother loved it
with more passion
than her only-born,
"It will bring us
shade, someday"
was all she said.

When I was six
it struggled
singular in the
wide space of
my father's hate,
its branches were
hooks holding
something hidden
in the air

When I was twelve
they were claw-
quills scratching
the shape of
our enemy's face

When I was sixteen
the wind struck back,
each limb scribbled
a single word:
                    pain

Then: spring and the
first feathering
bird-white blossoms
were the wings
of an immaculate shade

No matter for the
hundred stillborn
apples the frost
        got:

brevity is the
best passion,

and my mother's smile. . .

At nineteen:
lightning, but
half the tree
was spared, a
second lop-sided
feathering and back
to mere leaves as
each successive spring
my mother's memory
of blossom
        whitened

34

There are towns now:
Newark, Chippawa,
Queenston, and forts
and roads too,
and cattle graze
wary of sparrows
in their new pastures,
and Indians are no
longer amazed at
twelve-pounders and
gentlemen up to
their pressed trousers
in the man-made
mud of our streets:
only the trees
(in cautious retreat)
remain skeptical

"We are a country now"
so says my father,
his back imitates
the shape of the
rocking-chair he
pretends to love,
looking on the fields
we have cleared
together without love
or understanding—

35

and making the
ragged stump-fences,
the meagre green of
field and pasture,
the surprised cow
and one thunder-
struck apple—
making them fit
his only-dream
of home (he
hopes to die
before it fades
utterly)

Towns and roads:
a way in and
out—the guarded
eyes of others
born here too,
companions of
the countryless, but
some comfort too:
English beer and
the silken English
flesh of women

we plough and
turn and drown
in their incredible
green laughter

36

(the neighbour-girls
are white birches
bent lovely
with their labour
and slow-firm
growing, but
struck with a
double-silence)

"We are a country"
my father says,
"and you will know it
the day somebody
else claims it"

2

Tomorrow I turn
21, but
will this place be
birthground or
battleground?

37

We fight for a
few scattered clearings,
clumps of log-huts,
places with half-
savage names, our
own accents already
askew, more like the
Yankees we hate
than these British
regulars talking
among us, picking
their way down the
escarpment-edge like
crippled flamingoes

What country, then,
to be born into?

I have only the name
my mother gave me

and the place called
Upper Canada, and
I have now seen it
as far as Fort Detroit
and Chatham and York
and all the black
tree-spaces between
we call the woods

The Indians have a
hundred names for trees,
each animal is
known and dreamed,
is a tune for their
endless morning-songs,
their memories are
older than the animals

They have a hundred
tribes and each
has a name in
his own language:
Shawnee, Pottawatomi,
Ottawa, Muncee,
Wyandotte, Oneida:
these are syllables
no man not acquainted
with tree-creatures
could speak

and they are not afraid
to die because they
know the figure their
white-bones will make
against the other darkness

(out there, an
animal with an
Indian grin
dreams the
syllables of my
                    new name)

What deathgrounds then?

39

Today I saw
General Brock, his
costume fluttered red
as some exotic bird's,
but the eyes held me,
mirrors to picture
victims in

we were afraid
to be afraid

There are so many
Yankees, where do they
all live? what nation
lies over the river,
the horizonless lake?
what cities to crave
such generation?

From here, the
trees look the same,
what do they want
with ours? what
meaning for them
in our defeat?
                    my death?

40

But they come!
the badge of their
blue-coats glitters
in the neutral sun,
gun-fire and smoke-
shapes far below,
the farm-boy beside
me groans, we are
both surprised
at his dying, the
ease of it all. . .

at the signal
my rifle joins
the murderous noise
of its comrades

Afterward, corpses
on the green slope
stiffer than the
blue-starched tunics,
the cloth of their
strange country—

one wound is
mine, a spreading
red flower I
planted without rancour:

I look at the face—
it is mine, the
eyes have no colour

Brock is killed:
I witnessed the
bullet leave a
talon-print in the
scarlet plumage

blood-feathers
everywhere/the

brightest death

At Malden:
Captain Barclay,
one arm withered
since Trafalgar,
the other still
twitching, his
body too tired
to bend again,
throw its shield
of flesh over such
grotesque pain:

skin a
sheet of dried
blood-bark,
the charred eyes
will not reveal
the Enemy's face
or tell the dark
story etched inside,
(what strange countries
invade to taunt
and challenge)

We are commanded
to bury the dead,
pile the stumps and
half-legs, all the
bone-shrapnel in
a single grave,
a miniature clearing
nobody will name.

In the morning
the ships come in,
washed up red
and board by board
upon the aboriginal beach

Who will find
them? or care?

Lundy's farm:
war among the
tree-stumps, the
unbruisable ground

The setting sun
lays on their up-
turned heaven-
ward faces
such benediction
before death,
all our bodies
cupped with sun
the glass-edged
hate will break

43

Blue-coats,
smoke and black
grape-shot, the
purple bruise
on my left wrist,
scarlet sun-
set, the red
rage of my finger's
trigger of blood:

these are the
colours of my death

At last a
wound, the

pain flutters

bloodless/
butterfly
in the acid
   air

darkness, and
two dark wings
where my lungs
    are

Gun-flashes in
the night-sky
swim, waver,
flood with sun
this horror, the
slash of the blue
bayonet comes
so easy out of my
consenting flesh

My killer's face
pitted with blood,
ages while I
watch, will be
my last image,
I must smash
it, O it ex-
plodes in my hands
under the gun-butt
blows like a globe
of perfect porcelain,
all its tense
energies let
out and out

the darkness
will not hold. . . .

45

Sun lifting
out of the mist
the Falls makes
its delicious
noise out of
fresh light, the
day-dawn my
lungs lift to
my eyes sewn
shut with blood
sprout sudden

seeing   *here*
at Lundy's farm
the slaughter-ground
we bring our
hard breathing to,
the gift
of our living

3

Coming back:
my father buried
in the undiminished
shadow of the woods,
the wheat from two
seasons' planting
grown to the
grave's edge

46

what dream
swallowed him
before the last
seizing of light?

In the clearing
(my father's fields):
sun and sleep
the heat of a
turning earth,
larks in the
sweet grass,
the butterfly
bent lovely,
cows content
with small shade,
the domestic
sweep of wind
in the birches. . . .

My mother in her
living-room:
'We have apples
in the kitchen orchard"
was all she said

My eye goes out
to the wild apple:
its single branch
torn out of
dark angles
twisted with
decades of
accumulated pain—

7

it is a
young man's arm
supple and brave
beyond its years

it is an
old man's hand
grateful
      and
          brimming

And farther out
where the eye
forever ends:

      the trees, our trees

The colour of my country
is white and red

48

PART TWO

TECUMSEH: DREAMS AND VISIONS

I. KING PHILIP'S WAR

the English wear jelous that thcr was a gencrall plot of all
indians against English and the indians wear in like maner
jelous of the English. . . the report is that to the estward the
war thus began

the army first take al those prisoners then fell upone in-
dian houses burned them and killed sum men. the war began
without proclemation.

they solde the indians that thay had taken as aforesaied,
for slafes, but one old man that was Caried of our Iesland
upones his suns back. He was so decriped Could not go and
when the army tooke them upone his back Caried him to the
garison, sum wold have had him devouered by doges but the
tendernes of sum of them prevailed to cut ofe his head. . . .

but I am confident it wold be best for English and indians
that a peas wear made upone onest terems for each to have
a dew propriety and to injoy it without opretion or iusurpa-
tion by one to the other.

5th: 12m: 1675. Roadiesland

—John Easton

By this Time the Indians have killed several of our Men, but the first that was killed was June 23, a Man at Swansey, that he and his Family had left his House amongst the Rest of the Inhabitants; and adventuring with his Wife and Son (about Twenty Years old) to go to his House to fetch them Corn, and such like Things: he having just before sent his Wife and Son away, as he was going out of the House, was set on and shot by Indians; his Wife being not far off, heard the Guns go off, went back; they took her, first defiled her, then skinned her Head, as also the Son, and dismist them both, who imediately died. . . .

an Order was issued out for the Execution of that one (notorious above the rest) Indian and accordingly he was led by a Roupe about his Neck to the Gallows; when he came there, the Executioners (for there were many) flung one End over the Post, and so hoisted him up like a Dog, three or four Times, he being yet half alive and Half dead; then came an Indian, a Friend of his, and with his Knife made a Hole in his Breast to the Heart, and sucked out his Heart-blood: Being asked his Reason therefore, his Answer, *Umh, umh nu*, Me stronger as I was before, me be so strong as me and he too, he be ver strong Man fore he die.

Thus with the Dog-like Death (good enough) of one poor Heathen, was the People's Rage laid in some Measure, but in a short time it began to work (not without Cause enough).

—Nathaniel Saltonthall, 1676

52

While we were thus beset with Difficulties in this Attempt, the Providence of God wonderfully appeared, for by Chance the Indian Guide and the Plimouth Man being together, the guide espied an Indian and bids the Plimouth-man shoot, whose Gun went not off, only flashed in the Pan; with that the Indian looked about, and was going to shoot, but the Plimouth-man prevented him, and shot the Enemy through the Body, dead, with a Brace of Bullets; and approaching the Place where he lay, upon Search, it appeared to be King Philip, to their no small amazement and great Joy. This seasonable Prey was soon divided, they cut off his Head and Hands, and conveyed them to Rhode-Island, and quartered his Body, and hung it upon four Trees.

—Richard Hutchinson, 1676

53

TECUMSEH: TWO DREAMS

A DREAM

Cornstalk comes to
speak with the Long Knives,
it is summer and
Ellinipsico is with him
and Red Hawk has
left his arrows
in the meadow
below the square houses
the sun is on Cornstalk's
feathers the colour
the earth will be in the
new moon, his words
are rings of smoke
the meanings float
in there soft as
water with light
bending thru it
the voice is not
the sound of Cornstalk
but shudder of the
Drum-With-One-Tongue-
But-Many-Rhythms
the seasons of meaning
it takes our lives
to know them and
sometimes our death
the calumet speaks
its almost breathing words,
Red Hawk the warrior

and Ellinipsico
the boy-becoming
listen to the
gods's drum
inside the
small re-
ceding room
of their hearts

the white men
shout before their
hearts have heard,
they make their own
tongue-sound
(it is easy
to know them
or if they have
deeper drums
they do not hear
them or ever
let them out)

the sun is low
when the Long Knife
with the burning hair
scratches on the
paper with his
blue claw and
smiles as if
there were some
meaning to it
all

55

and then
the white-skin
comes
        his words
are bullets, they
do not carry
meaning, they
puncture it. . . .

Cornstalk stands
tall in the doorway
of the square house,
the sun holds up
the oval of his
face, he is
not looking at the
drum-beat of his
body knowing
it all comes
down to this
second, and Ellinipsico
shivering beside him
casting no shadow
in the square room
behind them where
Red Hawk trembles
in the chimney-hole,
soot scars him
long before the
lead hammers do,

the boy-becoming
wants to obey the
deer in his belly
but the father's hand
speaks: "The gods
have brought us both here
to share this moment,
who are we
to turn away?"

the guns tear
seven screams
in the Chief's skin
seven signs
my dream reads,
and the black gun
blows out Ellinipsico's
tongue and throat
and a last dream
of deer in the
deep home
of the woods, but
the flesh accepts
all stigmata
the air is
eloquent with the
wingbeat of
spirits and the
noisy death of
Red Hawk hacked
buttock-first
from his cowering-place

they chop his
body with their
swords, make a
black music
on his skin, you
can't see the
blood-boil in his
coward's mouth
nor the last
shame of eyes
shut with soot

O the anguish
of a death
without translation!

A DREAM:

My father's face
disintegrates, the
eyes sprung
from their grooves
their lifelong paralleling,
(dream-channels
to the old brain)
they are birds
uncoupled at
last one-winged
the ground has no
hold nor the air,

O no more
love or hate
mercy or revenge
light or dark:
without symmetry
there is no
                vision

twin cheekbones are
sundered by the
white man's curse
nostrils split
lips no longer
make the single
circle of a word,
the two-leafed
fern of the brain
divides its
perfect halves
so the dream and
the shadow of the
dream, the shape
and the shape of
meaning drift
beyond connection,
the blood gives up
its infinite branching
as the lung double-
pumps one cry
thru the crack
of his last lips,

59

it writes a
red word upon
his murderer's hands,
a branding-mark
for the dream
of a son
who must look
again and again
on the shattered symmetry
of this, my father's
perfect face

I did not see the deaths
of Cornstalk or my father,
but I dreamed them both:
and thus I know how they
happened, for my dreams
move in a slowed motion
like the heart does when I sleep
sending its small tunes of
sound through the drum-
tight blood   moves in a
time that lets me see
the image, the insignia
of their faces as death
relieved them from the
shame of dying. . . .

My dreams let me know
what signs are the same,
burned from the same wood:
the grain of their hate is a
smoking handprint of flesh. . . .

These after-images cool
in the quickening blood
but their shapes haunt
my wide-awake mind:
grieving skeletons
to hang my fury on,
to breed the creatures
who ate my mother's eyes,
to loose these hands
like jaws
upon the earth and the sky

(only man can
dream such creatures

    the gods
            are)

61

THE INFANT TECUMSEH

Elohama threw her anxious gaze through the deep shades of the surrounding wilds, but in vain—she listened in breathless stillness for the light footsteps of the hunter, but no sound was heard save the hollow murmuring of the gathering storm, and the wolf howling loud and discordant from his hills. Clasping her infant to her bosom, she sought the narrow path that wound through the wood, and determined not to return till accompanied by her husband. The night gathered dark around the wandering savage, and thunder rolled deep and heavy through the sky. In the pauses of the wind, a dying groan struck her ear. She followed the sound —it led to the body of Onewequa! A flash of lightning streamed across the stormy bosom of nature, and shed a livid glare on his convulsed features—Elohama sunk at his side.

"O my Onewequa, has thou fallen thus, and is there none to avenge thee? The arm of the warrior is broken since thou art laid low; but the young plant at my breast shall gather strength to crush thy destroyers.... Then let all thy petitions rest on the name of Tecumseh... then shall he be as a whirlwind and a storm, that scatter desolation and death.

—A story by A Lady from Indiana (*Canadian Magazine*, August, 1824)

62

AN INCIDENT

About the middle of May, 1792, a party of savages came upon a branch of Hacker's Creek, and approaching late in the evening a field recently cleared by John Waggoner, found him seated on a log, resting himself after the labours of the day. In this company of Indians was the since justly celebrated General Tecumseh, who leaving his companions to make sure of those in the house, placed his gun on the fence and fired deliberately at Waggoner. The leaden messenger of death failed of its errand, and passing through the sleeve of his shirt, left Waggoner uninjured, to try his speed with the Indian. Taking a direction opposite the house, to avoid coming into contact with the savages there, he outstripped his pursuer, and got safely off.

In the mean time, those who had been left to operate against those of the family who were at the house, finding a small boy in the yard, killed and scalped him; and proceeding on, made prisoners of Mrs. Waggoner and her six children, and departed immediately with them, lest the escape of her husband, should lead to their instant pursuit.

They were disappointed in this expectation. A company of men was soon collected, who repaired to the then desolate mansion, and from thence followed on the trail of the savages. About a mile from the house, one of the children was found where its brains had been beaten out with a club, and the scalp torn from its head. A small distance farther, lay Mrs. Waggoner and two others of her children—their lifeless bodies mangled in the most barbarous and shocking manner.

—Withers' *Chronicles*

GENERAL CLARK BURNS OLD PIQUA: 1780

The party I had joined was about entering the town with great impetuosity, when Gen. Clark sent orders for us to stop, as the Indians were making port holes in their cabins and we should be in great danger, but added he would soon make port holes for us both; on that he brought his six-pounder to bear on the village, and a discharge of grape shot scattered the materials of their frail dwellings in every direction. The Indians poured out of their cabins in great consternation, while our party, and those on the bank, rushed into the village, took possession of all the squaws and papooses, and killed a great many warriors, but most of them at the lower part of the bottom.

During the day the village was burned, the growing corn cut down; and the next morning we took up the line of march to the Ohio. This was a bloodless victory to our expedition, and the return march was attended with no unpleasant occurrence, save a great scarcity of provisions.

—Abraham Thomas, soldier

65

Light shakes
me, it is two
suns bigger than
both my eyes, they
do a red dance

Hurry   Hurry
a brother's voice
animal panic

I do not wish
to leave the
morning half in
me and half
out, but the
Long Knives are coming

I am running
ground is a
drum in my head
and two suns lock
in these sockets
the blood drifts
sleepward, the
half-morning of
green smells: fog
in the bottom-land
dew on the corn
grass and earth and
breathing hides

66

Hurry   Hurry
there's too much
light, I
see only the
red sun-dance
these green half-
dreams of morning,
I have always
let the day enter
my body find its
own balance of
light and shade
(it is bad to
ride the nightmare
too far out or in:

O let the sun
peel back the
cautious fogs, O
let all light be
crimson before the
bone-white noon:
a dance, a prelude,
a music of
early morning,
a sideways truth)

Hurry   Fire

wood-smell and
leaf-mould,
shadows where the
damp night is,
I turn back
into the sun
and it is noon:
bone-white over
the distant village,
the smoke makes
little word-skeletons
above each house,
for a moment they
emprison the flames,
are flagrant red
flowers, all that
power held under,
the vulnerable beauty
sundered like a
white-man's bomb,
like curses in a
language nobody knows

it is noon
and afternoon:
the creek coughs
with bodies and
loose blood,
the forest fills
us with its fear

Hurry   Hurry
the panic of women

68

but how do you leave
a birth-ground?
my dreams and night-ridings
and morning-songs are
merely other names
for the shape of things
a second way of
seeing what we are,
so how does one
say good-bye when
no word will do?

Hurry   Don't look back

I might have taken
that place with me,
half in each of my
two-sunned eyes,
in the deepest
remembering dance
(land-rhythms,
the signature of
seasons, this
poem of my
half-sung life)

but I turn
to the noon and the
afternoon and the
terrible sunset
west of the bottomlands
where Yankee firebrands
set the corn-rows ablaze:

they glow
like the fierce beards
of old men
(flesh sags
easier than brass:
but those charred stumps
will be a smouldering thumbprint
the sky reads as
warning, as prophecy—
    icons for my new
    nightmare)

With this hand
I draw the
first letter in a
bitter alphabet:

it is a vowel
and has no end

70

THE GNADENHUTTEN MASSACRE

In March 1782, between eighty and ninety men assembled themselves for the purpose of effecting the destruction of the Moravian towns. If they then had in contemplation the achieving of any other injury to those people, it was not promulgated in the settlements. They avowed their object to be the destruction of the houses and the laying waste the crops, in order to deprive the hostile savages of the advantage of obtaining shelter and provisions, so near to the frontier; and the removal of the Moravians to Fort Pitt, to preserve them from the personal injury which, it was feared, would be inflicted on them by the warriors.

Arrived among the Indians, they offered no violence, but on the contrary, professing peace and good will, assured them, they had come for the purpose of escorting them safely to Fort Pitt, that they might no longer be exposed to molestation from the militia of the whites, or the warriors of the savages. Sick of the sufferings which they had so recently endured, and rejoicing at the prospect of being delivered from farther annoyance they gave up their arms, and with alacrity commenced making preparations for the journey, providing food as well for the whites, as for themselves. A party of whites and Indians was next despatched to Salem, to bring in those who were there. They then shut the Moravians left at Gnadenhutten, in two houses some distance apart, and had them well guarded. When the others arrived from Salem, they were treated in like manner, and shut up in the same houses with their brethren of Gnadenhutten.

From the moment those ill-fated beings were immured in houses they seemed to anticipate the horrid destiny which awaited them; and spent their time in holy and heartfelt devotion, to prepare them for the awful realities of another world. They sang, they prayed, they exhorted each other to a firm reliance on the Saviour of men, and soothed those in affliction with the comfortable assurance, that although men might kill the body, they had no power over the soul, and that they might again meet in a better and happier world, "where the wicked cease from troubling and the weary find rest." When told that they were doomed to die, they all affectionately embraced, and bedewing their bosoms with mutual tears, reciprocally sought, and obtained forgiveness for any offences which they might have given each other through life.

—Withers' *Chronicles*

72

AN INCIDENT

One day in July a band of Indians composed of Shawnees with Tecumseh at their head, besides some Ottawas and Potawatomi came to my store—I have always enjoyed the confidence of these children of the forest—and asked me if I would go with them to Petite Côte, three miles beyond our picket at River Canard, to deliver a blow at the enemy. I could not refuse, since in that case I would have sunk very low in their estimation, so I answered them that I would gladly go with them. Accordingly, I made my preparations, not exactly those for a ball, but rather to try to exchange some English for American balls. . . . On reaching Petite Côte we arranged ourselves according to the Indian fashion on either side of the road, hidden among high stalks of corn so as not to be seen, and waited thus in ambush for the American cavalry. . . About three o'clock several fine squadrons approached. They were soon opposite the field where we were hidden, when suddenly from both sides came a furious discharge of musketry accompanied with arrow flights, which felled a large number of these men on their handsome mounts. Those who were not slain on the field begged for mercy but the Indians are absolutely deaf to all such entreaties, demanding nothing less than the death of their enemy. What carnage followed! Those with the slightest chance of escape tried to do so, some successfully, others less fortunate.

After a couple of hours the warriors returned from hunting the fugitives, having slain several of them. For the first time in my life I had taken part in a frightful carnage. I was filled with a horror of the war. Yet I must admit that the heart soon becomes hardened when these bloody scenes are repeated.

—Thomas Verchères, *Journal*

TECUMSEH: MEDITATIONS

I

a howl was my
first language—
shape of it
shuddering in
I was
        envowelled
in my mother's
arms endlessly
interwound with
sun splashed a
brilliant blood
on us both
we breathe the
earth's green
                air

O the hunger then
(I have known since)
was a bellows
my cries rode upon
the consonants bent
into words I willed
back bloody at a
world already
dying of wounds
and tribal hungering
in a thousand dialects

but I swallowed
my mother's tongue
whole, let it breed
the hollow vowels
I swelled with love
the consonants I
teethed upon, O
the words I need
to free the
night-creatures
crawling inside:
    insect-eyes
    and wing-buzz
    and six-legged
                dance

they are the figures
of my mother's dream
my tribe's history
the necessary nightmare

76

Then who is this child
on the green bank
with his head full of
M's—mother and wigwam,
the rivers: Mad,
Maumee, Miami and
Methoataske the
other name for the
woman whose mouth
was a song, and the
M of always-morning
in the M-shaped valleys,
or the big hump
in the middle of the name
his tongue makes hills
to climb over,
and Tecumapease
laughs her sister-
laugh when he
stutters on the
M   holds it un-
der: it shatters
like music on their
white teeth

3

But my name
is word as
well as tune

intricate lute
of syllable and sign
together they
breathe a melody,
a linocut of sound—
and meaning is a
wound on the wind

4

I was "crouching panther"
or "panther springing at his prey"
or when the wind blew
a certain way thru it
"celestial tiger"—even
"shooting star," "meteor"

(in the woods or
by the margin of a lake:
familiar eyes,

at night I
scanned the stars
for my namesake:

we were always
in disguise)

No wonder the
first sentence
I uttered was a
cataract that
murdered and soothed:

the World moved,
said nothing

AN INTERLUDE

In the family of James Galloway, who removed from Kentucky in 1797 and settled near Old Chillicothe, was an only daughter—the writer's grandmother. She was known then as a girl of remarkable mind and personality, both of which she retained in later life. This pioneer was himself a man of splendid mind and character and reflected his personality not only on his children and associates, but also very broadly on the early history of Greene county. It is not surprising, then, that Tecumseh, who frequently returned to his birthplace, should have formed a fast friendship with James Galloway and have been his guest at all times when in this vicinity. As the daughter, Rebecca, grew to womanhood this chief fell under the charm of her personality and the power of her mind and in that valley, amid all the beauty of forest and stream that nature can lavish on one landscape, he learned that "'Tis better to have loved and lost than never to have loved at all." In Colonel Houk's little brochure he quotes from Tecumseh's eloquent speech before General Harrison, and records the fact that although he arrived late at the battle of Fort Meigs on May 4, 1812, he stopped the massacre of Kentucky prisoners, who had been captured and turned over to the Indians for slaughter, and he upbraided General Procter for permitting it.

The use of excellent English, which distinguished Tecumseh's eloquent war and peace orations, reflected the careful teaching of Rebecca Galloway. She read much to him from the few books in her father's possession, corrected his idioms of speech and helped him enlarge his vocabulary in English. She read to him from the Bible and taught him the white man's belief in religion and future destiny, but the most signal service this girl performed to humanity was to

instill in Tecumseh, with every power of her artful charac-
ter, the fact that the massacre of prisoners after surrender,
and helpless women and children after capture, was against
every law and sentiment of humanity. History records that
he accepted and maintained this high ground in the years
which preceded his death at the battle of the River Thames.
I leave to the reader to infer how much love may have done
in this case for humanity.

—William Albert Galloway

TECUMSEH: DREAMS AND REFLECTIONS
OLD CHILLICOTHE, 1798

A dream:

skin whiter
than winter-feathers
of birds the sky
has stunned to crystal,
softer than snows
shaken from the
blue-spruce bough

a face in a
lunar landscape:
even the eyes
are immaculate moons
receding in the
fierce arctic light
of her gaze
            I

am the snow-goose:
stunned/shaken-down
made immaculate
by love. . . .

82

a dream:

blood-pink flesh
in brown hands/the
two-coloured weasel:
winter skin and
summer earth—
ermine's fur
diminishes snow,
the weasel's coat
gives back in spite
to earth each
spring the animals
eat their shadow:

    brown
           devouring
                    white

This Shakespeare made
words like the Manitou
casting pebbles to
fashion the universe

83

and this Hamlet
was not a man
(red or white) but
those syllables caught
on the page stiff
as a spider's web,
insect-tense
they are released
from *her* lips but still
this Shakespeare's words
out of the Dane's heart

I do not see the
man, the Prince,
but the faces of the
men he wished to be,
the words they must
say to themselves
(we are only the
words we can utter
or fashion in the
mouths of others)

And I feel your death,
the last sentence
in your throat was a
bloodflower we
both broke

84

Words were your
vengeance, you
longed for the easy
sword, the King's
blood in a chalice,
but you gave your
enemies epithets to
claim their diseases,
images to illumine
each crime, cast
them large into the
universe, we
see them even here
and now and still
the night-sky
glides on the bright
blood-pebbles
you and I and
Mitchimanitou
dreamed together

But your poetry fed
on its tutor's flesh,
you caught the
disease you named
with such precision
only silence
could cure it

What then but the
sword, the swift
one-syllable
                  word?

85

II. TECUMSEH BUILDS HIS CONFEDERACY OF WORDS (1811-12)

Earth has a voice
but no language,
its poems nudge
our simple sleep:

    we wake and
    tell the truth

86

PROCEEDINGS

Of a council begun and held near Urbana, Champaign County, Ohio, on Saturday the 6th of June, 1812, between his excellency *Return Jonathan Meigs*, esq. governor and commander-in-chief in and over the state of Ohio, and Ta-he, Sha-na-to, Scutush, Ma-na-ham, Dew-e-sew (or Big River), Cut-a-we-pa-sa (or Black Hoof), Cut-a-we-pa, Pi-a-ge-ha, Pi-ta-ha-ge, Na-sa-ha-co-the, chiefs of the Shawanoes, Ma-tha-me (or civil John) of the Mingoes.

His excellency addressed the chiefs, as follows:

My red brothers, chiefs of the Wyandots, Shawanoes, and Mingoes, I thank the Great Spirit, that has permitted us to come together where we can talk freely and sincerely. As father of the people of Ohio, who live as neighbours to you, I speak.

Brothers—Ever since the treaty of Greenville, we have lived in peace, and fulfilled all the promises then made to you. We wish always to live in peace with you; it is because we love peace, and not because we fear war. The Wyandots, Shawanoes and Mingoes, are brave nations, and brave men will not break their promises.

Brothers—Our great father, the president of the United States, whose eyes equally regard all his children, desires that you should live as we live, to raise your provision, and provide for your families.

Brothers—Open your ears: listen to what I say; I speak from the heart. Bad men and liars have endeavoured to break the chain of friendship. If you hearken to the deceiver called the Prophet, and the madman, Tecumseh, his brother, your skies will be cloudy, your paths will be dark, and you will tread on thorns. The pretended prophet has cheated some of the different tribes. He does not communicate with the Great Spirit; his counsels are foolish, and have stained the land with blood. The Great Spirit delights in seeing all his children live in peace, and smiles upon them when they do so; but he frowned on the Prophet at Tippecanoe, and his deluded followers were destroyed. *Beware, then.*

—Recorded by An Ohio Volunteer

PROCLAMATION

After thirty years of peace and prosperity, the U. States have been driven to arms. The injuries and aggressions, the insults and the indignities of Great Britain, have once more left them no alternative but manly resistance, or unconditional submission. The army under my command has invaded your country. The standard of the Union now waves over the territory of Canada. To the peaceable, unoffending inhabitants it brings neither danger nor difficulty. I come to find enemies, not to make them. I come to protect, not to injure you.

Separated by an immense ocean and an extensive wilderness from Great Britain you have no participation in her councils, no interest in her conduct. You have felt her tyranny; you have seen her injustice; but I do not ask you to avenge the one, or to redress the other. The United States are sufficiently powerful to afford every security, consistent with their rights and your expectations. I tender you the invaluable blessing of civil, religious, and political liberty, and their necessary result, individual and general prosperity; the liberty which gave decision to our councils and energy to our conduct, in a struggle for independence, which conducted us safely and triumphantly through the stormy period of the Revolution—the liberty which has raised us to an elevated rank among the nations of the world, and which afforded us a greater measure of peace and security, of wealth and improvement, than ever fell to the lot of any people.

If the barbarous and savage policy of Great Britain be pursued, and the savages are let loose to murder our citizens and butcher our women and children, this war will be a war of extermination. The first stroke of the tomahawk, the first attempt with the scalping knife, will be the signal of one indiscriminate scene of desolation. No white man, found fighting by the side of an Indian, will be taken prisoner— instant death will be his lot. If the dictates of reason, duty, justice, and humanity, cannot prevent the employment of a force which respects no rights, and knows no wrongs, it will be prevented by a severe and relentless system of retaliation.

—By the General, A. P. HULL
Head Quarters, Sandwich, 12 July, 1812

90

TECUMSEH SPEAKS BEFORE THE CHOCTAW

But what need is there to speak of the past? It speaks for itself and asks, Where today are the Pequot? where the Narraganset, the Mohican, the Pokanocet and many other once powerful tribes of our people? They have vanished before the avarice and oppression of the white man, as snow before a summer sun. In the vain hope of defending alone their ancient possesions, they have fallen in the wars. Look abroad over their once beautiful country, and what do you see now? Nothing but the ravages of the paleface destroyers. So it will be with the Choctaw and Chickasaw! Soon your mighty forests, whose wide-spreading shade you played under in your infancy, sported under in boyhood and now rest your weary limbs under after the fatigue of the hunt, will be cut away to fence in the land which the white intruders dare to call their own! Soon their broad roads will pass over the graves of your fathers, and the place of their rest will be blotted out forever.

The annihilation of our race is at hand, unless we unite in one common cause against the common foe. Think not, brave Choctaw, that you can remain passive and indifferent to the common danger and thus escape the common fate. Your people, too, will soon be as falling leaves and scattering clouds before the blighting wind. You too will be driven out of your native land and ancient domains as leaves are tossed in the wintry storms.

Before the palefaces came among us, we enjoyed the happiness of unbounded freedom and were acquainted with neither wants nor oppression. How is it now? Need and oppression are our lot—for are we not controlled in everything, and dare we move without asking by your leave? Are we not being stripped, day by day, of the little that remains of our ancient liberties?

Will not the bones of our dead be ploughed up, and their graves turned into fields? Will we let ourselves be annihilated in our turn without making an effort worthy of our race? Shall we, without a struggle of any kind, give up our homes, our country bequeathed to us by the Great Spirit, the graves of our dead and everything that is dear and sacred to us? I know you will cry with me, Never! Never!

Then let us join together to destroy them all, which we can now do, or drive them back whence they came. To fight or to be exterminated is now our only choice. *Which do you choose?*

The animals
have no words
and they dream
only of themselves:
the rabbit's flight
leaves a sign
in the snow the
fox reads with
his accurate eye—
when they meet
the story is over,
a signature of
teeth tells it all

So each animal must
be its own myth,
its body a badge,
its life one word
learned early and
never questioned

And though we know
Nanabohzo outwits
the too-sly fox
every time, yet
no-one has told
that legend to the
dead rabbit whose
one dream is lodged
in the fox's throat

93

TECUMSEH SPEAKS BEFORE THE MUSKOGEE

In defiance of the pale warriors of Ohio and Kentucky, we have travelled through these settlements which were once our beloved hunting grounds. No war-whoop was heard, but we have blood on our knives. The pale faces felt the blow, but knew not whence it came.

A curse upon the race that has seized our country and made women of our warriors! Our fathers from their graves reproach us as slaves and cowards. I hear them now in the wailing winds.

The Muskogee were once a mighty people. The Georgians trembled at their war-whoop, and the maidens of my tribe on the faraway lakes sang the praises of your warriors and sighed for their embraces. Now your very blood is white, your tomahawks lack an edge, you have buried bow and arrow with your fathers. O Muskogee, brothers of my mother, brush the sleep of slavery from your eyes. Once more strike for vengeance—once more for your country's sake. The spirits of the mighty dead complain. Their tears rain from the weeping skies.

Let the white race perish! They seize your land, they corrupt your women, they trample on the grass of your dead. On a trail of blood they must be driven back whence they came. Back, back, ay into the great waters whose accursed waves brought them to our shores. Burn their houses, destroy their cattle! The red man owns this country and the paleface will never enjoy it in peace. War now, war forever! War upon the living, war upon the dead! Dig their bones from the grave. Our country must provide no rest for a white man's bones. This is the will of the Great Spirit, revealed to my brother, his familiar, the Prophet of the Lakes.

All the tribes of the North are dancing the war dance.

Two mighty warriors across the great waters will send us guns, powder and lead. Tecumseh soon will return to his own country. My prophets shall tarry with you. They will stand between you and the bullets of your enemies.

Kill the old chiefs, friends of peace. Kill the cattle, the hogs and fowls. Do not labour—destroy the wheels and looms. Throw away the ploughs and everything American. Sing the song of the Indians of the northern lakes and dance their northern dance. Shake your war clubs, shake yourselves, and you will terrorize the Americans. The arms will drop from their hands. The ground will become a bog and mire them, and you may knock them on the head with your tomahawks. I will be with you, my Shawnee and I, as soon as our friends the British are ready for us. Lift up the war club with your right hand, be strong, and I will come and teach you how to use it.

Words are nets
of thinnest air
to catch the
subtle salmon

sometimes they come
with our breathing out
or spun crosswise
on the clenched teeth
become cocoons of
infinite anger

Without language
there is no
            catastrophe

and no poetry
to make peace
            with ourselves

96

TECUMSEH SPEAKS BEFORE THE CHEROKEE

I come to make a talk. To the great chief Junaluska and his people Tecumseh brings greetings.

Once our people were many. Once we owned the land from the sunrise to the sunset. Once our campfires twinkled at night like the stars of a fallen sky. Then the white man came. Our campfire dwindled.

Everywhere our people have passed away, as the snow of the mountains melts in May. We no longer rule the forest. The game has gone like our hunting grounds. Even our lands have almost disappeared. Yes, my brothers, our campfires are few. Those that still burn we must draw closer together.

Behold what the white man has done to our people! Gone are the Pequot, the Narraganset, the Powhatan, the Tuscarora and the Coree. They have put their sand upon them and they are no more. We can no longer trust the white man. We gave him our tobacco and our maize. What happened? Now there is hardly land for us to grow these holy plants.

White men have built their castles where the Indians hunting grounds once were, and now they are invading your mountain glens. Soon there will be no place for the Cherokee to hunt the deer and the bear. The tomahawk of the Shawnee is ready. Will the Cherokee raise theirs? Will the Cherokee join their brothers?

A dream:

My tongue is become
animal, a furred
body hammering
air into words:

>   otter's elastic bones,
>   black bear's quick
>   anger/slow strength,
>   a deer swimming
>   in grass, the length-
>   wise loon, the
>   sideways snake

they make a word-shape
the Darkwood demands,
that second when
the blood-mad
bones glow, the
skin translucent
lets the meaning
>   thru:

there is hope
and expiation

98

TECUMSEH SPEAKS BEFORE THE OSAGE

Brothers, we all belong to one family, we are all the children of the Great Spirit. We walk in the same path, slake our thirst at the same spring, and now affairs of the greatest moment lead us to smoke the pipe around the same council fire. We are friends. We must help one another bear our burdens.

Brothers, the blood of many of our fathers and kinsmen has run like water on the ground to satisfy the lust of the white man. We ourselves are threatened by this great evil. Nothing will satisfy the white man but our total destruction.

When the white man first set foot on Indian grounds, they were hungry; they had no place on which to spread their blankets, or to kindle their fires. Our fathers pitied their distress and shared freely with them whatever the Great Spirit had given his red children. They gave them food when hungry, medicine when sick, spread skins for them to sleep on, and gave them grounds that they might hunt and raise corn.

Brothers, the white men are like venomous serpents: when chilled they are feeble and harmless, but invigorate them with warmth and they sting to death their benefactors. The white people came among us feeble and, now we have made them strong, they wish to kill us or drive us off as they would wolves.

Brothers, many winters ago, there was no land. The sun did not rise and set—all was darkness. The Great Spirit made all things. He gave the white people a home beyond the great waters. These grounds he supplied with game and gave to his red children, and he gave them strength and courage to defend them.

Brothers, my people wish for peace, the red men all wish for peace; but where white people are there is no peace, except it be on the bosom of our mother.

But if we all unite, we will cause the rivers to stain the great waters with their blood!

III. TIPPECANOE AND AFTER

Our women and children were in the town, only a mile from the battlefield, waiting for victory and its spoils. They wanted white prisoners. The Prophet had promised that every squaw of any note should have one of the white warriors to use as her slave. . . .

O how these women were disappointed! Instead of slaves and the spoils of the white men coming into town with the rising sun, their town was in flames, and women and children were hunted like wolves and killed by the hundreds, or driven into the rivers and swamps to hide.

The Indians were defeated. Once my heart was very big, but Tecumseh filled it with gall. It has been empty ever since.

—Shabbona, Potawatomi chief and aide to Tecumseh

At one time from the farther end of Ball's field, a mile and a half this way, the road was covered with Indians, officers and soldiers, and horses, and from the Presbyterian Church, they must have judged our force at 3,000 men. We had about 1,000. A good many Yankees were killed. One Indian took two scalps. A young Cayuga had his arm and side carried away with a cannon ball, and another had a ball through his arm. Some of the musket balls came pretty close to us.

The cross-roads now are very strong. Dickson is expected here as soon as he returns from the expedition that has gone against Sandusky and Presqu'Isle with 1,500 Indians.

I wish George could bring a little starch with him for the frills of my shirts.

FROM SURVEYOR-GENERAL RIDOUT TO HIS SON AT CORNWALL

York, Sunday, 10th July, 1814

We have appearances now of very troublesome times. On Tuesday last, about four in the afternoon, General Riall crossed the Chippewa with his forces and attacked the enemy, whose numbers, as it appears by a letter written the same morning by Major Glegg, he was totally unacquainted with. The action continued about one hour and a half, when we were compelled to retreat over the Chippewa bridge, leaving many wounded. Major Buck, who commanded the place, is killed, Captain Dawson wounded, and all the men—two companies—killed, wounded or taken prisoners. The 100th regiment, commanded by the Marquis of Tweeddale, who had joined it that morning, has suffered greatly; of 600 men who went into the field, only 146 came out. The Marquis is wounded in the thigh and leg. He arrived here last night on one of our vessels, and is now at Judge Campbell's. Lieutenant Lyon, who attracted the notice of the Marquis by his bravery, and who was posted on our left near the Niagara River, only brought six out of the field. He was wounded near the close of the action by a grapeshot, which went through his right thigh a few inches above the knee, passing all the arteries, and the surgeon, on examining it was astonished at his wonderful escape. About 140 wounded were also landed here last night about nine o'clock, and five or six officers whose names I have not yet learned.

Captain Hey of the 100th is very dangerously wounded. The ball entered at the groin and came out in the opposite direction. Captain Sherrard of the 100th is also very much wounded in four places, yet there are hopes of him.

A few days will, I think, determine our fate.

104

TECUMSEH: LAMENTATIONS

The sounds I hear
in my dreams
are the voices
of the long-dead,
a man's cry
is not diminished
when his mouth is
stopped with a hatchet:
Wind carries it out
to every listening thing
and only when our ears
close from sadness
or neglect or the
intruding music
of our lives is a
man's death-song
taken back by the
trees, the quivering
air
    I
bend to with the
gift of dreaming. . . .

O hear the
death-cries of the
slain braves at
Tippecanoe, the
hum of opened
bones louder
than the bullets

that broke them,
the grieving of women
rearranging limbs,
faces the ground
might recognize

O hear the sound
the sky makes
when men grieve
quietly into it

O hear the cry
the wind gives
when women weep
softly under it

O hear the dirge
my body sings
when children call
out and out to
the sky   the wind,
these children without
the grief of men
the anguish of women,
without a name
for the white
man's death
devouring them

106

TECUMSEH'S LAST ORATION
THREE TRANSLATIONS

Fort Malden, October 1813

The speech of Tecumseh on this memorable day portrayed the energy of his character in the most animated and un-qualified colours. It was in the true Spartan style, laconic but expressive; and there burst forth the fiercer passions of his war-like soul. The language he made use of to the General Officer presiding, when the necessity for retreat was first urged was almost literally that ascribed to him in [my] poem. His eye absolutely beamed with the fires of his hot soul, and the warmth and thunder of his expression could only be equalled by the indignant character of his gesticulation. His speech acted like a shock of electricity on the hearts of every chieftain present; who, starting up to a man, and vociferating one universal yell, brandished their tomahawks in the most menacing manner.

—Major John Richardson

"Father—listen to your children, you see them now all before you. The war before this, our British father, gave the hatchet to his red children when our old chiefs were alive. They are now all dead. In that war our father was thrown on his back by the Americans, and our father took them by the hand without our knowledge, and we are afraid our father will do so again this time.

Listen! When war was declared, our father stood up and gave us the tomahawk, and told us he was now ready to strike the Americans—that he wanted our assistance; and he certainly would get us our lands back, which the Americans had taken from us.

Father, listen! Our fleet has gone out; we know they have fought; we have heard the great guns; but we know nothing of what has happened to our father with one arm. Our ships have gone one way and we are much astonished to see our father tying up everything and preparing to run the other way, without letting his red children know what his intentions are. You always told us to remain here and take care of our lands; it made our hearts glad to hear that was your wish. Our great father, the King, is the head, and you represent him. You always told us you would never draw foot off British ground; but now, father, we see you are drawing back, and we are sorry to see our father doing so without seeing the enemy. We must compare our father's conduct to a fat animal, that carries its tail upon its back, but when affrighted, it drops it between its legs and runs off.

Listen, Father! The Americans have not yet defeated us by land; neither are we sure they have done so by water; we therefore wish to remain here, and fight our enemy, should they make their appearance. If they defeat us, we will then retreat with our father.

At the Battle of the Rapids, last war, the Americans certainly defeated us; and when we retreated to our father's fort at that place, the gates were shut against us. We were afraid that would now be the case; but instead of that we now see our British father preparing to march out of his garrison.

Father! You have got the arms and ammunition which our great father sent us for his red children. If you have any idea of going away, give them to us, and you may go in welcome, for us. Our lives are in the hands of the Great Spirit. We are determined to defend our lands, and if it is his will, we wish to leave our bones upon them."

(Translated by John Richardson)

"But thou,"—and here his eye glanc'd fiercely round—
"Scarce dost thou know the foeman at thy gate,
Than, struck with terror, like some coward hound,
Thou shunn'st the fight, and flee'st thy helpless State;
Thy gallant youths, in combat foremost found,
Obey thy will, nor murmur at their fate;
But well their drooping hearts and heads proclaim
How much they curse thy fiat, and their shame.

"But since the blood runs coldly through thy veins,
And love of life belies the warrior's creed,
Go—flee—and leave to hostile swords these plains,
Then tell thy Father of the glorious deed:
Yet say, that well one native chief maintains
The faith he pledg'd, and on this spot will bleed—
For, by the Spirit of our mighty sphere,
Tecumseh moves not while a foe is near."

—John Richardson, poet

TECUMSEH: Brother! My people are before you now!
In the last war, the British father gave
Our chiefs the hatchet, and they fought for him;
But in that bloody strife the Long-Knife laid
The King upon his back; whereat he took
Our foes, without our knowledge, by the hand.
Again the Long-Knife warred upon the King;
Again our father handed us the axe,
With promise that our lands would be restored.
We have not shrunk from battle. We have fought,
And many of our people have been slain!
Our promise is redeemed! But what of his?
Oft have we heard you, boasting of him, say
He never would withdraw from British ground.
Yet, neither asking nor advising us,
We mark you now preparing to retreat—
Afraid to even see his enemies!
My brother, you are like a lusty dog
Which proudly curls its tail upon its back,
But, when affrighted, whips it 'tween its legs,
And runs for life! Why should you meanly flee?
The Long-Knives have not yet defeated us
By land, nor is it certain that your ships
Are captured on the lake; but even so,
First fight, and, if defeated, then retreat!
But brother, if you will not fight, you hold
The arms our father furnished for our use.
Give these to us, and you may go in peace.
My people are in our Great Spirit's care!
We are determined to defend our lands,
Or, if he wills it, strew them with our bones.

—Charles Mair, poet

TECUMSEH: A VISION

I want to fashion good words forever,
stretch my body into a continuous sentence,
humiliate the air with speech, break
the chronology of my people's despair,
sew them green stories, chronicles of hope,
weave a new history from our twin beginnings:
we shall see our own shame and the
white man his——he will smile and
give up his books, his bellicose
reading of the world's working-out,
my myths will eat him, page by page,
into silence——decoded, he will be free
at last to utter those poems that have
no need for the curvature of words. . . .

MORAVIANTOWN

Tecumseh entered the battle of the Thames with a strong conviction that he should not survive it. Further flight he deemed disgraceful, while the hope of victory in the impending action was feeble and distant. He, however, heroically resolved to achieve the latter or die in the effort. With this determination he took his stand among his followers, raised the war-cry and boldly met the enemy. From the commencement of the attack on the Indian line his voice was distinctly heard by his followers, animating them to deeds worthy of the race to which they belonged. When that well-known voice was heard no longer above the din of arms the battle ceased.

—Henry Howe, Ohio historian

Scarcely had he expired. when a band of lurking enemies sprung upon the warrior, and scalped him. Not satisfied with this, they absolutely tore the skin from off his bleeding form, and converted it into razor-straps!!! If the Indians have sometimes treated the Americans with cruelty, they, at least, were not Christians; and as for simple scalping, it has been a custom with the natives since time immemorial—the scalp being considered merely as a war-like trophy; but when men, professing to call themselves Christians, and calling themselves enlightened, can descend to the commission of indignities such as were offered to the body of Tecumseh, they certainly have but little reason to inveigh so bitterly against Indian barbarity and treachery; and many Kentuckian Americans have I heard boast of having obtained a part of the warrior's skin.

—Major John Richardson

TECUMSEH/LAST THOUGHTS ON THE THAMES

At last
they have given up
the centuries-long
pursuit of my bones—
grim souveniring
(Indian skin
tanned and braided
in a girl's hair,
my scalp is
leather for some
Yankee museum,
my tongue a
tobacco every
Long-Knife yearns
to chew on,
dip their fingers
in my interminable
blood, whisper
my name over and
over as they lance
the quivering female)

They would not leave
me graveless,
needed this proof
of their courage,
or maybe they
really did know
our bones belong
to the place that
gave them length,

that my name would
survive the cursing
of present voices,
my skeleton hang
like a smoking
question-stroke
over these death-grounds,
over these last
few counties
I now call my
home, my grave

Of course, there is
nothing to find:
my corpse was not
cached in some
animal's burrow,
nor cut up and
broadcast under the
ceremonial moon,

when the bullet
struck my heart
split once like a
milkweed pod
and we floated
myriad and free. . . .

116

Yet, I cannot leave,
that is my burden,
for 160 years
my spirit has found its rest
here in these southern counties
in the last field before Moraviantown.

At first it was much
like my birth-ground:
the Thames (despite an
English name) found
its own way thru the
wooded bottomlands,
easy and effortless it
brought the seasons down
over my thousand bones
and for a while
it might have been the
Wabash   Ohio   Miami....

In the town of Chatham
children play ball
on a green field
which bears my name
(their laughter is a
music I remember:
let me call out—
the game goes on)

117

And there are streets
and learning-places
inscribed with the
letters of my name,
and I have heard them
strangely on the lips
of school-children
telling of the battle,
of the Chief's bones
hidden beneath a
cellar, a barn-floor,
a forged grave-mark—
and some of them
strangely are sad,
and one too old
for his age
sits in a
cramped room and
draws my name
over and over
'til there's no
more white
on the white
                    page

TECUMSEH: DREAM AND VISION

This dawn-light is
ember-thin, it
quickens and
                    dismembers

me

I am fading
into the bleached
bone-beauty of

                    poems

I am everywhere
photographed in the
darkest rooms

I am the
passionate statue
in each of your parks

I am the
poet in his pure

                    air

(remember and
                    beware)

119

BIBLIOGRAPHY

In one form or another I am indebted to each of the following works, and especially to Glenn Tucker's fine modern biography.

Auchinleck, Gilbert. *A History of the War* [1812], introduction by H. C. Campbell. Toronto, 1972.

Edgar, Matilda. *Ten Years of Upper Canada.* Toronto, 1890.

Howe, Henry. *Historical Collections of Ohio.* Cincinnati, 1888.

Lincoln, Charles H., editor. *Narratives of the Indian Wars 1675-1699.* New York, 1913.

Mair, Charles. *Tecumseh, A Drama and Canadian Poems.* Toronto, 1926.

Quaife, Milo Milton, editor. *War on the Detroit* (Journals of Thomas Verchères and James Foster). Chicago, 1940.

Randall, E. O., editor. *Ohio Archaeological and Historical Collections,* X (1901-02). Columbus, 1902.

Richardson, Major John. *Tecumseh, or The Warrior of the West.* London, 1828.

———. *Richardson's War of 1812,* edited by A. C. Casselman. Toronto, 1902.

Thompson, David. *A History of the Late War.* Niagara, 1832.

Tucker, Glenn. *Tecumseh: Vision of Glory.* New York, 1956.

Withers, Alexander Scott. *Chronicles of Border Warfare.* Cincinnati, 1895.

PART ONE

THE PIONEERS: FIRST QUESTIONS
SECOND THOUGHTS

For Anne and Kate and John